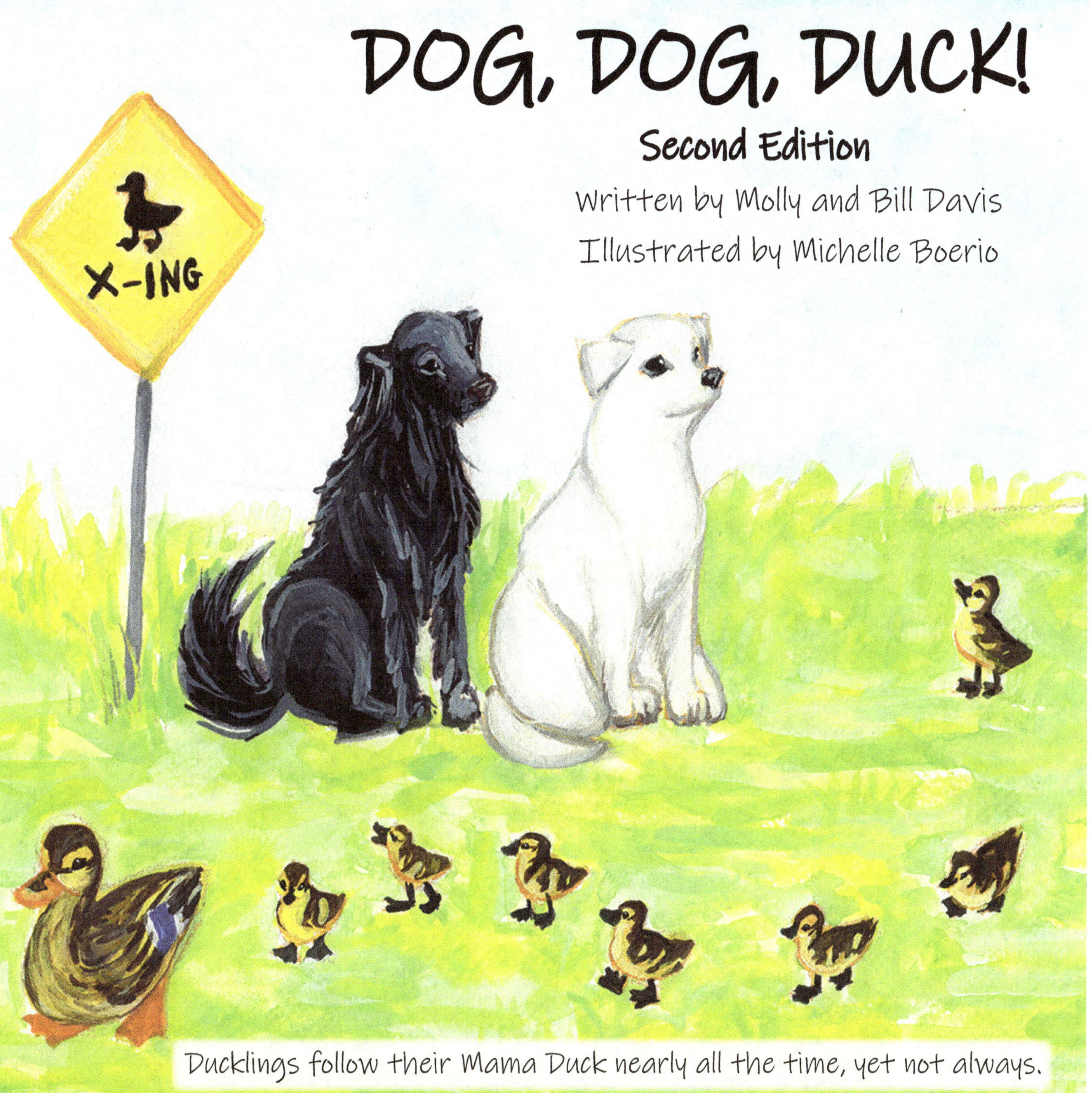

DOG, DOG, DUCK!

Second Edition

Written by Molly and Bill Davis

Illustrated by Michelle Boerio

Ducklings follow their Mama Duck nearly all the time, yet not always.

DOG, DOG, DUCK! Second Edition.
Copyright © Mary C. Davis, Readitagain LLC, Columbus, Ohio
All rights reserved. Published May 11, 2024.
Library of Congress Control Number 2024909313
ISBN 979-8-218-42033-8
Printed in the United States of America

Dedication
To Vivienne Kmietsch and Rustin M. Moore
for their exceptional care of and commitment to animals

After Vivienne fed all the animals, everybody in the barn followed her outside.

On that April morning, Whinnie, a black mare with two white socks and a white star on her forehead, and Abey, an all-black horse, trotted near the old tree whose roots sprawled across the muddy ground. Every day, these horses trotted, whinnied, and neighed their way down to the creek and back to the barnyard.

Showlow, the black dog, and Nali, the white dog, ran around and splashed in puddles. The other animals moseyed around the barnyard.

Spring had sprung up in rural Ohio.

2

Suddenly, Showlow and Nali stopped and stood—still as still could be—near bare shrubs with tiny green buds on the ends of skinny-sticked branches.

Showlow and Nali barked. Barking more, they ran to Vivienne, then ran back to the shrubs. Something was going on, Vivienne thought as she followed her dogs.

"What's the matter, friends," Vivienne asked. The dogs barked and danced around near the shrubs.

Vivienne saw seven eggs in a pile of last autumn's leaves and dried, brown grass.

"Oh, no! she shouted.

"These duck eggs are all alone with no Mama Mallard in sight," she yelled out to her animals.

"The sun's coming up and shining through the shrubs' bare branches and onto the eggs in the nest. We must not disturb or touch the eggs now. We must wait to find out whether Mama Mallard returns to her nest. If we disturb the eggs before she comes back, she might abandon the nest."

As the sun began to inch down at day's end and, having seen no signs of Mama Mallard all day, Vivienne thought the only chance for these eggs to hatch would be by keeping them warm. So, she brought a large cardboard box and set it down near the shrubs.

"Mama Mallard did not come back. We don't know how long she had been sitting on the clutch of eggs before she disappeared or how long she'd been gone from the nest. Mama Mallards usually only leave the nest for about one hour a day," she said. "We don't know what happened to her, and we must try to help," she added.

Vivienne brought some hay from the barn and spread the hay inside the box. Her steady hands picked up the eggs, one at a time, and gently placed them in the box. Vivienne carefully carried the treasure box of eggs into her house to keep them warm and safe from any predators.

It takes 28 days for mallard ducks to hatch once the Mama Mallard begins sitting on the nest. Vivienne didn't know when to expect the eggs to hatch or even if they would hatch. She peeked into the box frequently to watch for signs of life inside the small eggs. Showlow and Nali lived in the white house with Vivienne and helped her keep an eye on the eggs.

4

After only four days at Vivienne's house, the eggs started to crack and rustle around in the box. When Showlow and Nali peeked in the box, they saw cracks in a few eggs. In two days' time, all the baby ducklings had pecked and scootched out of their shells. They huddled their tiny, soft bodies together. "We don't know how long the Mama Mallard had been away from the nest. Coming from the wild, it is a miracle that all seven eggs hatched in this box in our home," Vivienne thought to herself. "Pretty soon, we'll take our friends outside," she told Showlow and Nali.

Early one sunny morning when the seven baby ducklings were a couple of weeks old, Vivienne took the treasure box containing them outside. She placed each duckling, one at a time, onto the dew-sparkled grass.

"When baby ducks don't have a Mama Mallard nearby, they might follow others," Vivienne explained to her barnyard friends.

6

Before anyone knew it, the ducklings started to follow Showlow and Nali around the barnyard.

Sometimes, the horses, pigs, and chickens joined the parade. Other times, they wandered all over the place just for the joy of it.

One morning, a whisp of wind touched one of the ducklings. A tuft of yellow down floated up, down, and all around, like a dandelion fluffy.

The down tuft landed right on one of Whinnie's shiny black legs. Whinnie leaned her beautiful head down and said, "Why, thank you, friend!"

Vivienne went to the hardware store and brought home a children's rubber swimming pool in her truck. She plopped the pool down in the grass and filled the pool with water.

The ducks hopped right into the pool and immediately began playing, splashing, and "ducking" their heads under water looking for food. The ducks' webbed feet could paddle and glide all around the little pool. As the ducks got bigger, Vivienne brought home two more pools.

The ducks started flying short distances, oftentimes in the early morning or early evening, from the porch and back.

Vivienne and her animals spent the drowsy days of early summer in these happy ways.

9

As summer settled in, the ducklings' yellow down disappeared. The ducklings grew bigger and had brown feathers. They had skinny looking, yet powerful legs and feet for swimming. The ducklings hatched with black feet. Over time their feet turned a brownish color. Much later their feet can be a bright orange color and only as big as the palm of a five-year old child's hand.

One late-June evening, however, a few of the young ducks flew away. Just like that. They came back the next morning and that evening, a few more ducks flew away with them. All the ducks came back in the morning. That evening, those six ducks flew off and never, ever returned to the barnyard.

Only one duck stayed behind. Vivienne called her Ducky.

Showlow and Nali leaned their noses down and gave Ducky a friendly sniff.

"Glad to have you with us for as long as you like," Showlow told Ducky. Nali yipped to let Ducky know she was welcome to stay.

Ducky followed Showlow and Nali everywhere they went around the barnyard.

11

One afternoon inside the white house, Showlow and Nali stood on the window seat and looked out the bay window. They saw Ducky all by herself in the barnyard.

Suddenly, Ducky's beautiful brown body with a brilliant blue patch on each wing, flew up and hovered eye-to-eye with Showlow and Nali on the other side of the bay window. Ducky quacked and quacked and Showlow and Nali barked and barked as if they were communicating with one another.

Seeing the three friends and hearing quacks and barks, Vivienne said to nobody in particular, "They seem to be talking to each other." She opened her kitchen door to the outside and stepped aside.

Ducky waddled into the kitchen and over to the window seat. She flew right up and settled herself between Showlow and Nali.

After that first day in the white house, Ducky came into the house most afternoons to take a nap with the dogs. She often shooed Showlow or Nali off one of their dog beds and nestled herself onto the bed.

When summer stopped being summer, Showlow and Nali romped around outside in the golden autumn days. Ducky waddled clumsily behind them as the three friends paraded through the barnyard.

Every day, all the animals that Vivienne rescued were taken care of and safe. Together they all spent such peaceful days in this lovely and safe haven.

Late one autumn afternoon, everybody heard the wild ruckus of a flock of ducks and saw them flying overhead. A few days later in the evening, even Ducky flew away. Just like that.

The next morning, Ducky returned to the barnyard and had breakfast with the chickens. That evening, she flew away again.

Yet the next morning, there she was, eating breakfast with the chickens. She flew away again before it got dark that night.

Do YOU think Ducky will come back again for breakfast?

15

She did!

The next time everybody in the barnyard heard a wild ruckus, Vivienne pulled on her tall, black rubber boots. Vivienne, Showlow, Nali, and Ducky ran out of the house and joined their other friends in the barnyard.

17

Everyone saw a flock of ducks, flap-flapping their wings and quack-quacking their loud voices through the cold, crisp, cloudy air. Then, the flock of ducks flew off and faded into the sky's enormous clouds.

Vivienne and the animals stood in silence as they watched the ducks disappear into the clouds. Not a whinny, cluck, oink-grunt, bark, quack, or Vivienne's voice muttered among the friends who stood in the brittle, brown grass on that November afternoon.

"I wonder whether our six other mallard ducks flew away with the flock of ducks. We don't know," Vivienne said to all who were there with her on that day.

After that day, Whinnie would look at the parade of the three friends, then stomp and paw the ground with one of her white-socked feet. Whinnie would neigh with joy to everyone in this peaceful place, "DOG, DOG, DUCK! DOG, DOG, DUCK!"

All around our wonderful world, every ordinary day is full of extraordinary lives of different species—animals and people—living peacefully together and enriching each other's lives.

DUCKS' FOLLOWING BEHAVIOR, WHICH IS CALLED IMPRINTING

Imprinting is a form of learning whereby a young animal fixes its attention on the first object it has visual, auditory, or tactile contact with and thereafter follows the object as its mother, where it gains a sense of species identification for life. This is common in nature especially among wild birds, and mallard ducklings are no exception as they imprint on both their mother and fellow hatchlings.

They do not become visually imprinted to their hen until after departure from the nest and this visual component of maternal imprinting leads to active following once they depart the nest, whereas early in postnatal development the hatchlings are more visually attractive to one another than to their mama duck.

Imprinting allows baby birds to understand appropriate behaviors and vocalizations for their species, which aids in their safety and immediate- and long-term survival. Imprinting also helps them to identify with other members of their species, so that they may choose appropriate mates later in life.

The timing of the imprinting varies among species, and some birds are more susceptible to imprinting inappropriately on human caregivers for reasons not fully understood. Thus, it was important that Vivienne take steps to prevent the ducklings from imprinting on her to optimize the chances of a successful return to the wild and survival.

Because the ducklings' eggs were moved from their nest and hatched in a deep box, they did not have visual or tactile contact with Vivienne during the first couple of weeks, and thus they seemed to imprint themselves on one another rather than on her.

This story is a wonderful example of how mallard ducklings were successfully hatched and reared without becoming imprinted on the human caregiver, allowing them to survive, thrive and return to the wild when ready. Of course, there is always one in the group, this time Ducky, who may have imprinted a little more on Vivienne and the dogs than the other ducklings.

Ducky still flies off in the evening and is gone throughout the night before returning in the morning where she eats and interacts with her barnyard companions. Where she goes at night is a mystery and will probably remain.

Rustin M. Moore, DVM, PhD, Diplomate, American College of Veterinary Surgeons
Dean, College of Veterinary Medicine
Ruth Stanton Chair in Veterinary Medicine
The Ohio State University

Words that might be new:

Clutch — a group, a bunch

Down — the early soft feathers on a duck

Glide — move along in a smooth way

Neigh — a sound horses makes

Ruckus — a loud noise

Tuft — tiny bit, often of something incredibly soft, like feathers

Waddle — walking with the body moving around with each step

Whinney — another kind of sound that horses make

Webbed — skin between the toes to help ducks walk and swim

Some other children's picture books about ducklings:

Delano, Marfe Ferguson. *Ducklings*

Magloff, Lisa. *Watch me grow: Duckling*

Moore, Eva. *A True Rescue Story: Lucky Ducklings*

Sexton, Colleen. *WATCH ANIMALS GROW: Ducklings*

Suen, Anastasia. *Spot BABY FARM ANIMALS: DUCKLINGS*

YouTube.Com

Go to YouTube.Com and type in "ducklings following dogs" to watch fun videos of ducks following dogs.

Vivienne Kmietsch riding Whinnie. Rescued Animals Living at Vivienne Kmietsch's as of April 2022

Six mallard ducks that hatched in April flew away in late June and never, ever returned to the barnyard

Ducky, the remaining mallard duck, was still returning to Vivienne's each morning as of March 2023

Horses: Whinnie and Abey (pronounced like Abe Lincoln, with an ee sound at the end)

Four Sheep: Vivienne calls the Lammels, except for one black sheep, who is Sarah

Dogs: Nali (pronounced like Denali), Showlow (named for Show Low, Arizona), Rusty, Dino, Troy, and Scooby

Cats: Peaches, Troix, Tree, Marie, Bunsie, Paw Paw, London, Habani, Chloie

Pigs: Bailey and Rainey

Leopard Tortoise, named Kruger

Sun Conure, named Sunny

Two parakeets, no names yet

Chickens, no names yet

Old Rooster, James

Photo of Ducky with Showlow, Nali, and Troy. Nali on the floor.

Acknowledgement

With gratitude to Dean Rustin M. Moore
for his invitation to work on this book,
for his excellent explanation of imprinting,
and for his teaching, recommendations, and editing approaches.

Bill and Molly Davis wrote and edited this book together: Molly, mostly the writing; Bill, mostly the editing. Before their retirement in 2020, Bill taught physics, and Molly worked as a writer, both at their alma mater, The Ohio State University. Molly's other children's picture books include: *A Birdie Told Me, Second Edition*, illustrated by Katie Riccardella. In addition, the following three books were illustrated by Carrie Lacey Boerio: *Tired of Naps!, Where in the World is the Moon?*; and *RESOURCE GUIDE for Where in the World is the Moon?*, which was developed and compiled by Denise V. Carskadon and Anne C. Albrecht. They live in central Ohio.

Michelle Boerio is a visual artist and educator from Columbus, Ohio. She loves to make art that highlights the weird and wonderful parts of the natural world. She earned a BFA from The Ohio State University with a focus in Painting and Drawing and an MA in Museum Education from the University of the Arts in Philadelphia. Currently, she divides her time between making art and teaching art with students of all ages.

www.ingramcontent.com/pod-product-compliance
Lightning Source LLC
Chambersburg PA
CBHW060219120726
48004CB00008B/1873